Living on His Income

{Cover photo - My mother-in-law. A classic housewife, around 1959.}

Living on His Income

Remembrances and Advice for the Christian Housewife

By Mrs. Sharon White

The Legacy of Home Press
puritanlight@gmail.com

The Legacy of Home Press
ISBN-13: 978-0692221075
ISBN-10: 0692221077
Living on His Income – Remembrances and Advice for the
Christian Housewife

Author – Mrs. Sharon White

Contents

Living on His Income

Remembrances

Grandmother Dorothy

I grew up in my grandmother's house. She was a Christian housewife all of her married life. Her home was originally a beach cottage that Grandpa built up and expanded over time. The home was in a suburb of Boston. It was a lovely place. As they reached the twilight years, they needed help, so Mother agreed to move us all in. We three children and Dad took over the second floor. Grandpa Frank and Grandma Dorothy lived in a little apartment on the lower floor. Grandpa had set it all up and fixed it nicely for his beloved wife. She was a semi-invalid by that time and in a wheelchair. Frank had taken care of her for richer for poorer and through all phases of their married life. They had 4 children and 11 grandchildren. The house was on a charming acre of land. There was a garage with a wood stove and a nice garden near the back. We had lilac bushes by the side of the house. This was Dorothy and Frank's home. I was privileged to grow up there.

I watched Dorothy work from her wheelchair. She worked at the kitchen table helping to prepare food. Out on the side porch, a clothesline was attached near the window. Dorothy could wheel over there and hang clothes. She could cook in that chair and manage the home. She could sew and knit while chatting with visitors. She would hold grandbabies and delight in the family. My Mother did most of the caretaking of Grandma after she became bedridden.

One day, it seemed, in the blink of an eye, Frank passed away. Then sometime later Dorothy joined him. I watched my mother lean over the casket to give her Mama one last kiss goodbye. She whispered, "*I love you Mom.*" I was 11 years old.

Looking back, I remember so much more. Dorothy was the center of the home. Family was everything. They lived during an American era that valued the wife at home. This was just how it was done. It was not questioned. A man provided for his family, and mother kept the home.

Frank's house was paid for through his lifelong work as a laborer. He worked at the Shipyard. Dorothy was allotted a portion of that money to feed the family. She would make a list of all the things she needed, and Frank would do the shopping. Dorothy made that money last. She was not frivolous and she never lived above their means. In those days, a big family dinner was served on Sunday afternoons. This included meat and a dessert. These were all made from scratch, of course. A homemaker took pride in her ability to nourish the family with her own cooking. This was being a good steward of the resources put into her hands. Society helped keep life *family - centered* by keeping places of business closed on Sundays. Families were free to relax and enjoy home, and a quiet day of rest. Dorothy and Frank made that home a happy place to be.

Weekday meals were more common, and included little meat. Bread was served, and fresh or canned vegetables from the garden. Processed and packaged foods were not common in the family kitchen. There was no such thing as prepared breakfast cereals, until Cheerios came on the scene in the 1940's. You would not find a freezer full of frozen dinners or cabinets packed with store bought convenience foods. Mother made the food. These were made with such things as flour and sugar and eggs and milk. Frank's family was from Italy. Dorothy, of course, made foods he liked best. She made her own pastas and sauces. In those days, Mother's cooking was a blessing and a comfort to the family. No "thanks" went to Kraft foods or the Kellogg's company. "Thanks" went to Mother. Husbands and children wanted to rush home for dinner because Mom's home cooking was wonderful. Nobody cooked like Mom!

What did Dorothy do for a living? In those days, no one would ever ask such a question; because her job at home was sacred. She was Frank's beloved wife and the Mother to their four children. She was there. She made that place a home by her presence.

Great Aunt Rita

Frank's brother, Chet, lived across the street. He and his wife Rita had a cute little house. We children would be playing in the yard and see our Uncle Chet and Aunt Rita driving by in their car to do shopping or errands. We would always wave. After my grandparents passed away, my great Aunt and Uncle were like grandparents to us. I remember walking down their small, woodsy driveway. They would be sitting on the side patio. Chet had all kinds of antique cars and collectibles all over his property. There were wind chimes near the side door. Rita's house was like a dollhouse. It was compact with a tiny kitchen, livingroom, hallway and 3 bedrooms. This was where they had raised their 3 children. Rita would invite me into the kitchen and give me a cold drink or an ice cream cone. There were windows surrounding her kitchen, making it almost like a glassed in porch. On the other side of the house, there was a dinner bell. She would ring this to call her children or grandchildren home from the private beach across the way. The couch had a homemade afghan over the back side. Like most men of the day, Chet had his own special chair. This was where he could rest from a hard day. Rita would bring him a cold drink. She took good care of her husband. They lived a very simple life and were always around to welcome visitors. From today's standards, their home was very old looking. But in those days, prudence in spending and saving, and enjoying a clean home was a way of life. The American dream was to own land and a house. One would make do and work there to make it clean and pleasant. This was where one rested from one's labors, and where one offered neighborly hospitality. No grand house of today could compare to Chet and Rita's humble little beach dollhouse.

My Mother

Back at home, my father worked and mother stayed at home. She was a housewife for many years. She continued the traditions of thrift and cleaning that Dorothy taught her. We had daily and weekly cleaning to do. Mother and we children kept the house nice. Dad worked as a machine mechanic and came home in the late afternoon each day. He paid the bills and provided the way for us to enjoy the lovely old home. We had a china cabinet in the corner of the livingroom. I used to dust the cabinets and shelves each week. I was in awe of something very special, which I knew used to belong to my grandmother. The old piano was just below a large mirror at the front of the livingroom. We children enjoyed many hours of sitting on the bench, looking through music sheets and trying to play. We had a large rug over linoleum on the floor, which kept the house looking home-like and humble. I never realized how thrifty and careful my mother was with Dad's income, until I was visiting the homes of school friends. I saw new houses, and modern fixtures. I saw an abundance of varieties of food in the freezer and cabinets. While we children did not know hunger, we did not have such a vast amount of convenience food available in our kitchen at home. Mom made our dinners from scratch. We occasionally had ice cream, but it was only one choice of flavor. Or, in the summertime, Dad would make ice cream in a special bucket with dry ice and a crank.

All of we children went to school and worked to earn our spending money. There was no such thing as allowance in those days. I had never heard of my friends receiving spending money either. I am sure it may have happened in some homes, but not in our circle. We never would have thought of such a thing. Babysitting and yard work were the main jobs available to children in our neighborhood. When I was 12 years old, and all through most of my teen years, I had a babysitting job each Friday and Saturday night. There were a variety of families I worked for. I would get anywhere from $5 to $12 for the night. I would often start at 5 or 7 in the evening and finish by 1 a.m. Someone would always drive me home at the end of my shift. These nights out were for the husband and wife. I had a favorite family I worked for. They had 2 little school age girls who were so sweet and easy to take care of. Their parents would go out to dinner, or go to the country club one night a week. They were an older couple and very devoted to each other. The money I earned babysitting was used for treats like getting pizza or going to the movies with friends. I would also buy my own nail polish, brushes, clothing, and whatever else a young girl would need.

In those days, parents bought their children new clothes in August. You got a small wardrobe and new shoes for the coming school year. That was it until Christmas. You got a new robe, or nightgown, and some new outfit, along with a few gifts. Most presents were practical along with a few nice things you had hoped for. Then in the spring, at Easter time, we children got a new outfit for Church. Of course as the school year ended, we each received a small summer wardrobe. We only bought extras throughout the year, from money we children earned ourselves.

We did not receive gifts or get spending money unless it was our birthday. Today, it seems, many American children get a present or cash every week, or whenever they go to the store. It lessens the appreciation in children and tends to spoil everyone. We expect more. A great virtue is lost - patience. When we know we have to wait for a holiday or birthday for something new, we take better care of what we have, and are willing to work hard and wait.

The culture was beginning to change around this time and some of the homemakers were taking on part time jobs in the evenings. This was in the 1970's and 1980's. In my neighborhood, this was often for social reasons. My grandmother and other housewives of their time had been very involved in the Church. Families were pulling away from this religious social outlet in the 1980's. I often wonder if this was why some of the wives in my neighborhood decided to start working outside the home. These mothers got all dressed up and worked in a local upscale clothing company. My mother was one of them. This was not until one's

Living on His Income

children were older, and they were left in the care of their Father. This was after Mother made dinner and the house was put back in order. Most children went off to do homework, watch a little television with Dad, and then went to bed. I had never heard of a daycare until a preschool float was in our town's 4th of July parade, when I was a teenager. I could not imagine why a preschool or daycare was needed and had to ask my Mother. (I personally only knew of one "career mother" then. She was a registered nurse who married late in life and had a couple of sons.)

There were still housewives in the area. They depended on their husbands as providers and were happy and content at home. I call them housewives because to me, it is a life-long term. These were married women who stayed home and didn't have jobs. This was where they wanted to be. I had friends whose mothers were happy as housewives and it was comforting to see them always home, always around, and always happy to be hospitable. They were there to help us when a need arose.

However, one of the saddest things in our community was when a sweet, dear Christian lady was abandoned by her husband. She was forced to work to raise her two sons. She told me, years later, that all she ever wanted was a lot of children and to stay home, but her husband stole that dream from her. She was a lady with great faith and did what she had to do. I understand this type of thing is very common now, in these modern days, and it is very sad. Those who are fortunate to have a husband who is willing to provide are blessed and privileged!

Perhaps this is why I knew enough, at the age of 17 when my boyfriend proposed marriage to me, to say I had only one condition. That was for me to be allowed to be a housewife and to never have to get a job. He agreed and we were married a year later. He has always kept that promise to me, no matter what our circumstances. I believe part of his willingness to do this was his own upbringing. His mother was a lifelong housewife and an incredible example to me.

My Mother – in – Law, "Meme"

My husband's mother was known to us as "Meme." This was the French term for grandmother. Even though she was in her 40's at this time, she already had a couple of grandchildren. The first time I met her, my boyfriend and I were walking towards the yard. She had long hair which shone in the sunlight. She was wearing a housedress and was tending her flowers. When she saw us, she called out to her son, "Pick up your girl and carry her across the yard. I just put fertilizer all around. I don't want her to have to step on it." So I was picked up and gallantly carried into the house. What a wonderful first impression of my soon - to - be- mother in law!

During our married years, we visited Meme many times. She was so peaceful and content at home. She had a small flower garden. The birds were often chirping sweetly in her yard. She was always home and rarely went anywhere. She took excellent care of the home. Through the trials of her grown children and grandchildren, I saw wisdom in how she mothered. I learned patience and how to appreciate a lifelong marriage. Her husband took excellent care of her. They did not live rich lives. They did not have wealth. They lived a regular life without any hint of extravagance. They were very careful with money and always had food.

Papa (my father - in - law) had one vehicle. He worked at a job, and did all the errands. He would do the grocery shopping once or twice a week. Whenever Meme would run low on household items (like paper towels, soap, milk or bread), she would write a list and leave it on the refrigerator. She often added things to the list as the days went on. Sometimes items would completely run out before Papa had a chance to get to the grocery store, but she never once complained. She was not worried. She knew how to get by, to make do, and to do without. Meme knew that Papa was tired from work and didn't always have a chance to stop at the store on his way home. Often errands were done on his days off. Meme respected this and lived around his schedule.

There was peace in their home. There was also respect and understanding. Of course no home is perfect and relationships have their trials, yet these waves on their life did not change the way they lived. They were an example of a secure home and a secure family. They could get through any battle together. This is key. All couples have disagreements and differences. But this never changed their family. For nearly a quarter of a century, through good times and bad, through financial needs and financial gain, my husband's parents were a shining example to me of a beautiful home where Mother is always there caring for the home, and father provides. It was a classic example of a traditional family and I was blessed to be a witness.

Living on His Income

My Experience

In the mid - 1990's working from home started to become popular among housewives. Mothers were encouraged, through magazines and newspapers, to earn money. They were told they didn't have to leave their children. They could earn some of the living and stay home at the same time. We Mothers were exposed to more and more teachings on earning money, and less on thrift, homekeeping and motherhood. There was an explosion of schemes and genuine opportunities to make money. This desire for money took up so much of our attention that it was almost as if we didn't have as much time for holiness, prayer, keeping our marriages intact, or on devoting our entire lives to our homes and children. We had hearts that were being divided between making money and learning to live on our husband's provision.

In the beginning, some of us were taking care of other people's children in our homes. We housewives would think, "Well, I am taking care of my own children anyway, what is one or two more?" I was always home to do this. Over the years I have taken care of many children while mothers worked. It was not ideal and I didn't always like doing it, but at the time, this was what was happening.

Later, as homeschooling came on the scene, we mothers would start little businesses in our homes that we could do with our growing children. This taught them valuable lessons in business, customer service, budgeting and so much more. In our home, we have had several little companies running from time to time. There were weekly yard sales, sewing shops, and baking and cooking companies. This, for me, was never to earn the living; it was part of our homeschooling. Any money that came in often went to the children to teach them money management skills. They used their earnings to buy clothes, books, and to have spending money. From the beginning, my husband and I agreed that he would provide the money, and I would take care of the family. I never wanted to interfere with our agreement, or complicate it, by earning money to "help him" or to "supplement his income." I was happy to live on what he made, riding out the seasons of good times and bad.

At one point in my family, my husband and I owned a general store in a rural area. We lived in an apartment above the store and ran the business with our five homeschooled children. The building was set up as if it was one big house, so we lived where we worked. We did this for four years and then retired from such work.

Those years we had businesses were the most exhausting of all. However, I am so grateful to my husband that he has kept his promise to me, and I have never had a job since the day we got married almost 3 decades ago. I have been home and very content here.

I do have to say, that for most of my married life, I have not earned money. I have tried to be diligent with the resources my husband has provided, despite my failures. I cannot even describe how very precious it is to be here, to be at home, and to make this place a refuge for all who enter.

Of course I would never say it is wrong for a housewife to earn money from home. But I will say that the example of my grandmother and mother-in-law is the ideal. The lives of Dorothy and Meme are the most beautiful and peaceful to me. As I go through this life, I learn these lessons and I constantly strive to live more and more like the housewives before me. Their influence and way of life was priceless.

Remembering these housewives comforts me and provides such peaceful memories. There is something about being taken care of and trusting someone to provide. It brings out a child - like faith and trust in a housewife. It brings a gentleness and a sweetness. It reminds me of our Heavenly Father. By living on my husband's income, ideally, this is similar to how I live on the income God has provided our family. My husband is the provider. I am the housewife. We are both grateful and blessed.

Advice

Living on His Income

Standard of Living

There were some old sayings one would hear in previous generations concerning marriage. Things like, "I want to marry for love and not money." Another good one was, "I am the wife of a poor man." Often, when a man from a lower social class would court a wealthier girl, he would feel unworthy and incapable of providing a life for her that she was accustomed to. Many of the rich girls wouldn't go near a poor man. They didn't want to have to "sweep their own parlours," or "do their own washing." They wanted maids and cooks. They wanted nice clothes and beautifully decorated homes. They wanted to live in high style and live a high life. What could possibly entice them to adjust their standard of living to marry a poor man? It would be a life of burdens, financial worry, and living in want. This is how it has always been in the world.

To complicate matters, many women now have careers and work to buy the things they want. They don't depend on their men anymore. Sadly, American culture has changed so much that few men are even willing to work to earn the living. It is considered an "outdated responsibility."

But the man who is willing to take care of his wife and children must have a woman who will adjust her housekeeping to his income. These are often godly wives who want to live the old paths, the old ways. They want traditional homes where faith in God is the foundation. They want to follow the Biblical order of the woman being the keeper of the home and the man providing the living.

Homemaking on his income is becoming a lost art. We don't need granite counters in our kitchens. We don't need double sinks in the bathroom. We don't need new houses or new cars. There are so many different ways to live that we can find some type of housing to live within our husband's money.

There are cabins in the woods. There are mobile homes. There are apartments and simple houses that have not been lavishly modernized. In the old days, a good woman would say to a prospective husband, "A furnished room with you is all I need." It was possible for a couple to rent a room in a reputable boarding house and live in just a room. That was the starter home. As time went on, the wife would be frugal and prepare her husband's meals, be a good housekeeper, and make his income go far. Later, they would be able to move on to a larger home, perhaps an apartment or a small house. This was how working class families with low incomes used to live. It is admirable and instructive!

Many wives of today want to have a higher standard of living. They want to run out and earn some of the money so they can have more material things. Some even want to switch things around so they earn the money while the husbands stay at

Living on His Income

home! This is not the Biblical way, no matter how much the world says it makes financial sense. The world is not our counselor.

I once heard a preacher say, "The world is diametrically opposed to God's way." Why would we follow the crowd and live their way?

"A tent or a cottage, why should I care?

They're building a palace for me over there;

Though exiled from home, yet still I may sing;

All glory to God - I'm a child of the King."

- A hymn from, "Soul Stirring Songs and Hymns," page 221, " A Child of the King."

The Vision of Home

There are those who are called to the mission field. They may go to school to learn how to work and live within a new culture. They give their whole lives and their time to the mission work. These families are required to gather support for their basic living needs. Once the finances are in place, this is what they must live on for the year. They are so devoted to their work for the Lord, they may sacrifice large sums of income they could have earned had they chosen another lot for themselves.

In like manner, a wife has a mission field in her own home. She is called to a post in the home. This is where she is stationed. This is the culture in which she lives. She does it with the financial support of her husband.

She most certainly should learn how to run a home, how to cook and clean. She should know how to mend and to do those little touches of home economics that make a home. This ought to be a lifelong study so that she can keep her little mission house running.

Women today are taught to stay on the fence. They are taught to keep one foot in the career world, just in case things don't go well. They are told they can always work part time or just a little so they remain current and necessary in the working world. How can a missionary housewife leave her post and still give all her time and attention to the home? This would be a divided calling. There are two masters here. One is the mission. The other is the outside job.

The home is so important that a wife is needed there. Across the land, there are empty homes left untended. I once read that American homes are the loneliest places during the day, because no one is there. All the mothers are out working jobs. The home is the most neglected place in our culture. It has become the unreached mission field. Many wives are needed there. Few are willing to take it on. We need more training in home economics and more training in living on a small income. We need more wives willing to take on this incredible work, to makes homes into bright lights of godly living, in the midst of a dark, cold world.

We need housewives who will not waver from their post. They need to have courage and kindness, and to stand proud despite any storm or trouble, much like the missionary workers overseas. We need brave women who have a vision of home as the mission field.

In The Sweet Service of the Master

If left to our own devices, we would be grumpy, miserable, complainers. This is just human nature in an imperfect world. That is why it is so important that we seek holiness. The light and peace of the Lord shines through those who love Him and have their faces set towards Him. We need to be diligent in prayer and the reading of the Bible.

In these modern days, it is easy to hear the Bible and to hear good sermons. We have CD players and computers. We can find old fashioned sermons online and on tape. There are even CDs of people reading the Bible. I have a set of CDs of the King James Version of the Bible being read by Johnny Cash. I love it! I use it rarely, when I am sick or having trouble finding a way to read on my own.

We can seek holiness throughout the day, by the culture we set up in our homes. We can also guide our children in the old paths. This is one of the greatest benefits of being a housewife in a Christian home. Our being home, as a godly influence, has an impact on our children. Doing our daily work in the home, while living out God's laws, teaches character and values to our family.

Making a house a home is one of the most beautiful jobs we could ever do. My mother could make us all feel at home no matter where we were. Whether on vacation, visiting family, or in the car, we knew that being together was an extension of home. Mom always did those basic chores that kept things neat and pleasant. She also taught us to do them too.

One thing that has always puzzled me was to get into a messy car of another family. Some had trash, junk, and garbage all over the floors. I couldn't understand it. I realize that children are messy. When we are out on errands, sometimes trash can accumulate. But when we get home, Mom can say to one of the children, "here is a bag, go clean out the car." And to another one, she might say, "I want you to set the table for dinner." Each child doing a little bit of work, makes it easier for Mother. But it also teaches them to do those little services in the home that make our surroundings nice.

When my children would grumble and complain, I taught them that doing this work was like doing a "mitzvah." That is a Jewish term for doing the commandments or good deeds. When we do mitzvahs, we are doing God's work. It brought a cheerful smile to the children's faces and made the work more meaningful.

All that we do in the home, done heartily for the Lord, is a sweet service. We can surely be a cheerful homemaker when we have proper times of rest, work, prayer, and quiet time with the family.

The Content Wife

How many of us have complained to our husbands that we wanted new clothes, prettier furniture, or a new set of fashionable curtains. I know I certainly have. Often this happens when we have visited a wealthier family and admired their decor. Or, we may have seen a beautiful magazine photograph of a lovely home. Sometimes commercials or television programs make us envious of another way of life. We start daydreaming about things we don't have and that are out of our financial reach.

I saw an old episode of "I Love Lucy." The family's apartment was beautifully kept and nicely furnished. Many homemakers of today would love to have their home look like the Ricardo's! But in one episode, Lucy and her neighbor Ethel went to "The Home Show." Their husbands knew they would come home wanting all new furniture. They were certainly right! This is natural and something we need to fight against.

A valuable life is not about materialism. It is about doing good with the resources we are given. It is making the best out of what is put before us.

Most of our money is best used to further the kingdom of Heaven. Yes, that is charity work, missions, supporting churches, and caring for the less fortunate. While there is nothing wrong with having nice things, it is time consuming and destructive to always want something better or different than what we already have.

In my childhood home, we had humble furnishings that were practical and pretty. I can't recall anyone in my family redecorating. We kept things clean and neat. If something wore out or was outgrown, it was carefully replaced when that was possible. This always took time. Sometimes a year would go by before a need was filled. Families in those days knew how to get by and make do. We knew that money was mostly for basic needs and not frivolity. We knew that nothing happened immediately. Patience, as the old saying goes, was a virtue.

I can still remember the old wallpaper on our living room wall. It was so home-like and familiar. If I still lived there, I would keep it just as it was, replacing things only as absolutely necessary. We had an old dining room table. There was a drawer on one side where we kept the silverware. This sturdy table was never replaced or "upgraded." If we already had a bureau or an end table, why would we go out and buy a new one? Just because we wanted a change? It just wasn't practical. It was not something we would have thought about. This must be contentment: Happy with the housekeeping we have been provided with, and making the most of what we have.

Unworldly

Values and ideas change with each generation. Often we have no idea that our thinking has been corrupted or mixed up with modern philosophy. One way to correct this is to step back. It is sort of like going up to a mountain to pray.

They say that if you stop consuming sugar for 30 days, when you go back to taste it, you will not like it. You will realize it is bad for you. You can do this same thing in a spiritual sense. I realize we cannot step out of the world and live completely isolated and holy for a month, but we can certainly make an attempt based on our situation. If we took a break from television, newspapers, magazines, worldly books, and visiting places of the world, this is like taking a step back. It is like a Sabbath or a vacation from the world and its problems. Husbands and children do not have to be affected when Mother has her spiritual fast. We just stop what we ourselves are doing, while they continue as normal. How that works for each family, even if it is only a small effort, will be different. But it will make a difference in our thinking.

In "The Sword of the Lord" newspaper, I read a sermon by a gentleman who talked about a happy Christian home. He said that his parents didn't necessarily have to tell him that a certain way to live was unbiblical. He and his siblings, as they grew up, figured it out on their own in an interesting way. His parents lived such a happily devoted life to the Lord, that when the children went to worldly paces, they sensed an incredible difference. They wanted to have homes like Mother and Dad did. They wanted happy Christian homes where the family were all out for God and dedicated to His work. This is "unworldliness."

We are in the world, but not of it. Touch not the unclean thing and God will receive us. This means that each and every step we take towards holiness and godly living will take away the desire, the tangling up, with worldly wants and worldly living.

The steps to heaven take us away from this imperfect world. A sweet housewife will make an effort every day to clear away the clutter and debris of worldliness that keeps trying to invade her heart.

Living on His Income

Homemade

Just about every home used to have a hand crocheted afghan on the back of the couch. This was made by mother. I remember making a pretty blue one while I was pregnant with one of my babies. As I crocheted, I prayed for that child. Each stitch of the hand brought peace to my heart while I created something homemade for my family that I loved.

Every baby, in my generation, used to get a set of handmade sweater, booties, and a bonnet. These were in neutral colors, like peach or white because we didn't know what the baby was going to be until after birth. Those beautiful homemade clothes were charming and precious. Dressing our babies in a crocheted bonnet and sweater was like taking care of a beloved doll.

Today, I am hearing that new mothers don't want the homemade gifts. They want store-bought, name brand, and fashionable clothing for their babies.

Something is being lost here. It is something very precious. When items are handmade with love and prayer for the family, it is like passing on a great virtue to the next generation. It is keeping up with the art of home.

I still remember sewing a little dress for my first baby girl. I had walked to the little sewing shop in town and selected a simple pattern. I bought the "notions" I needed and the fabric. While my baby was playing or napping, I would work on her dress. I was so proud and happy to make her something with my own hands.

One December, I had become friends with a mother from our church. We were both expecting babies. She already had one child, and I had two little girls at the time. We visited each other and went on a few outings with our children. We talked about homemaking, cooking, baking, and sewing. I was working on a set of matching dresses as a special surprise for my little girls. I also wanted to trim the collars in lace and make matching hair ribbons. I have always considered myself an amateur and did a lot of my sewing by hand - using a basic plain stitch. But this time, as I worked on those dresses, I received valuable advice from my friend, who was a talented seamstress. We each had our little projects we worked on when we visited each other. Then back at home, I remember staying up late after the girls had gone to bed, and sewing happily. I couldn't wait until Christmas when I could give the dresses to my children. They were so happy to receive them. Those girls had seen me, over a period of weeks, making the clothes for them. They saw sacrifice and love as I worked. This was a great blessing to all of us.

We can also have homemade decorations around the house. Some can get flowers from the yard and bring them to the table, putting them in a simple vase or glass bottle. We can cut simple scraps of fabric to make tie - backs for an inexpensive set of curtains. Some mothers with limited money available to them might take family photographs and tape them to pretty paper to set up on a hutch or decorate the walls. Homemade touches make a home special and inviting.

It doesn't cost very much to create a homemade atmosphere. It is a beautiful way to live in a humble Christian home.

Dependent on Him

Sometimes husbands complain about financial matters. They might have a rough time at work and start venting. This is very common and happens in all homes. Often, however, a wife of today might be tempted to jump up and offer to help ease his troubles. She might say she'll get a job to help out. This is one of the most common ways wives of today end up leaving the home. I realize it is very tempting today and I want to just reassure those lifelong housewives that this is not always the best route.

I used to explain to my sister that when my husband would have a problem at work, I would be sitting in a rocking chair knitting and say, "I am sure you will figure it out, dear." I would continue to knit and rock, quietly and sweetly. He would calm down, the moment would pass, and all would be well. This is the type of thinking that will be heckled and scoffed at by most women of today. But the truth is, this little scene is the norm in my home and in my grandmother's generation.

I am going to be bold here and say that regardless of how much this reaction to my husband's financial troubles will make people mad, this is what it means to be dependent on him. It means that my husband's role is to provide the living. My job is to take care of the home and family. I will not switch roles with him. That is not my place, nor do I have any inclination to do such a thing.

Financial troubles come to every home and they have in every age. They come and go just like the stock market rises and falls. This does not change our places in the home. In the old days, Dad would pack up the family and move to a less expensive place, or he would seek out another job. When a family was in dire straits, sometimes the extended family would take them in for a time. No one would ever expect the wife to leave the home and family to take on a man's job of providing.

A wife and mother was cherished at home, and was protected. No one wanted to wear out her strength or take her time away from making home a peaceful haven. No one wanted to lose her constant prayers and godly influence. Mother was valuable and needed at home.

God has lessons and plans in store for my husband. He is working through his life (just as he works through mine). I will not jump up and interfere with this by stepping in and trying to take over my husband's part. He has his work to do. I have mine. I need to believe in my husband, stand behind him, and trust that he can overcome any obstacle that comes his way. I need to let God work through my husband, stand back, and continue to do my job at home. This builds great faith and an incredible testimony in the home.

Living on His Income

Of course, if my husband were to say to me, "finances are going to be extra tight for a little while. I need you to cut back on some of the bills." I will gladly do what I can to economize, lower the utility bills, and be more creative with our kitchen resources. We will put off certain expenses and go without some things. This is how we work together to get through the rough times.

Living on what one can afford is becoming a lost art. In Scripture we are told that we are to seek God first and all the things we need will be added unto us. Seeking God and His ways is an incredible journey. I have had so many instances of great financial miracles that God has blessed us with. I will share with you a few things that have happened just this past month.

1. While sorting papers for my husband, I came across some savings I had forgotten about. This was for a few hundred dollars. My husband and I were both shocked. We put it aside and just waited. By the end of the following week, the money was used for a trip into the next state. A relative had passed away and we were able to attend the funeral.

2. After the birth of one of our grandchildren, I came home and found a check that had come in the mail. It was for more than one hundred dollars. It was a refund from our health insurance policy, that I had no idea we were entitled to. This money greatly helped with extra expenses during the week with the new baby.

3. Here is just a little thing - I needed a few items from the local drug store. As the cashier rang up my items, I expected it to total more than $6.00. She told me it cost $1.20. I couldn't believe it. I was just delighted! This is a little blessing, but these little things are like smiles from heaven.

4. I received a donation one afternoon and was so grateful. I didn't make any plans of what to do with the money. I have learned to wait and see. The next day, my old glasses broke, but I was able to order a new pair, thanks to that unexpected money.

I have noticed, over the years, that sometimes the Lord lets us "get ahead" as the world would say. Money comes in and is put aside for "a rainy day." But then it is needed for life. Most people would scoff and complain. But I know better. The Lord has shown me, over these many years, that the money he sends is for His purposes. Lately, it seems, that He trusts me enough that he is sending the money before the need arises. Because He knows I will not run out to the nearest mall and spend it.

Depending on my husband for our income, is a great test of depending on God for my life. It is an incredible act of trust and faith, and most certainly of patience. A housewife at home, faithfully living for God, devoted to her family, is a shining light of holiness the world desperately needs to see.

Living on His Income

The House Account

When I was in my early teens, I bought a little cash book from the local drug store. It was in the office supply section. It was blank inside, other than all the fancy lines designed for bookkeeping. I used the left side of each line to write the date. The middle was for a description. And the two sections on the right were for either income or expenses.

As I earned money from babysitting, I wrote down which family I took care of, and how much I made. I also wrote a record of my spending. Today, all these years later, I smile when I see the entries. Some are "bought pizza: $5.00" or "bought pocketbook: $5.00." I can also see a trip I took with my sister to California when we were in our teen years. Here are some of those spending entries: "Pens and Postcards at Spruce Goose: $8.21" and "breakfast at airport: $9.00." I also love to see that I bought croissants and cokes!

I can see how my values and spending habits matured with time. When I started working at a regular job, I was paying my tithe and supporting missions. I was also paying car insurance. This was at the age of 16.

I can see a short history of our spending when I was married with one baby. My husband's weekly allowance was a mere

$30! We spent $85 on groceries that same week, and an additional $55 when my husband received a bonus.

My bookkeeping was sporadic in those years. It has revived in the last decade. I have a larger, ledger style book where I keep track of my household spending. This is to record the history of our lives. You can see so much of your life by how you use your money. It is also wonderful to remember the events in our lives, by seeing where the money went.

In the last few years, I have bought sleeping bags, flashlights and care packages for Christian camp. I have bought extra food for special holiday events. I remember these things when I read over some of my ledger book entries.

It is one thing to keep and maintain a monthly (or weekly) budget. This is very important. It is also another thing to actually write down every penny spent. This can be part of being a good steward of the money provided.

Personally, I don't write down the bills I've paid in my ledger book. You won't see a note saying I paid the electric bill or the car insurance. Those are regular bills listed in my budget. I only write down the money I spend that is designated in the budget as the house account. This is for groceries, charity, tithe money, outings, clothing and whatever life brings. I also want to say that I don't keep track of my husband's personal spending. He has an allocated amount and that is just like one of the bills to me.

Living on His Income

I also tend to have one of the children help me. Usually it is my youngest son (a teenager). He sorts my receipts and records the entries in the ledger book. It teaches him many skills on so many levels.

When I write down the entries, or have one of the children do it for me, I tend to be more careful with my spending, knowing that it will be recorded.

Puritan minister Jonathan Edwards' wife, Sarah, did an excellent job of keeping track of household spending. She left a fine example to us of a prudent wife. I love this quote describing her:

"It was a happy circumstance that he could trust everything to the care of Mrs. Edwards with entire safety and with un-doubting confidence. She was a most judicious and faithful mistress of a family, habitually industrious, **a sound economist, managing her household affairs with diligence and discretion.**" from *Marriage to a Difficult Man- The Uncommon Union of Jonathan & Sarah Edwards* by Elisabeth Dodds

In these modern days, some like to use computer spreadsheets. Others like to keep track of categories so they can see from month to month, or year to year, how much was spent on groceries, utilities and the like. The way we keep track of our spending is a personal choice. But for me, I would much rather sit at a table or desk, with my old fashioned ledger book, and write down the things I did with the money. I don't do this to see how much went where. I do this to see how we lived from day to day, and to remember.

Edith A. Barnett, in 1894 (London) wrote a book called *"Primer of Domestic Economy."* Here is a quote from this document - "Whether the income be small or large, certain or uncertain, the good housewife will keep an accurate account of her income and expenditure." She also wrote this: "Probably women as housekeepers spend the greater part of the money that is spent in the world."

How well we manage the house account, affects our entire family. When we avoid impulse buying, and take great thought before parting with money, we have the power to help keep the home stable and secure.

The Next Generation

"I have been young, and now am old, yet have I not seen the righteous forsaken, nor his seed begging bread." - Psalm 37:25

When my children were little, I read from a set of books called, "Uncle Arthur's Bedtime Stories." These were full of faith - building stories about family and prayer. My children loved the lessons! They heard me read about children who learned to share, how they helped their neighbors, and how they prayed to God for their food.

Over these many years, my children have seen me as a housewife. They have seen us go through times of riches and times of near poverty. Through it all, we have prayed for our needs and walked the road that God has led us on. The children have watched us wait for the things we wanted or needed.

In this modern day, we see fewer and fewer wives at home. We see them heading off to careers when the children are in school, or once they've grown and moved out. We don't see housewives at home like we did in grandmother's day.

Most of the time, it is about money. But the old ways of the mother at home is such an important example to both the younger mothers and to our growing children. We need Titus 2 women to be the shining influence to the coming generation.

Today, as I was looking at my old cash book. I noticed an old newspaper clipping I had put in there from the 1980's. It was from a local Cape Cod newspaper. It contained a beautiful poem for Mothers. It sums up what we need to hold on to, and what we mothers need to keep showing the generations to come by our example at home:

"A house should have a cookie jar

For when it's half - past three

And children hurry home from

school

As hungry as can be -

There's nothing quite so

splendid

In filling children up

As spicy, fluffy ginger cakes

And sweet milk in a cup.

Living on His Income

A house should have a mother

Waiting with a hug

No matter what a child brings

home,

A puppy or a bug.

For children only loiter

When the bell rings to dismiss

If no one's home to greet them

with a cookie or a kiss!"

- Author unknown

Living on His Income

Appendix

Living on His Income

Practical Resources

"Good Old Days" Magazine

This will encourage you and help you understand the way life used to be.

"Mama's Bank Account" by Kathryn Forbes.

This sweet story will show how a traditional mother and housewife took care of the home. It also shows the beautiful way in which the family paid the weekly bills.

"The Complete Tightwad Gazette" by Amy Dacyczyn

For practical instruction on frugality.

"Aunt Jane's Hero" by Elizabeth Prentiss

This book was published in the 1800's. It is a fictitious story that will show the most beautiful humble home and a precious Christian marriage.

Living on His Income

"All of God's Children Have Shoes"

(An article by Mrs. White to encourage the old fashioned housewife.)

Many years ago, a dear old mother taught her children great faith in God. She had no education and raised the family in material poverty. She was one of many, many mothers in similar circumstances throughout history. This dear lady, in particular, loved the Lord with all her heart. She taught the children songs which cheered them on their daily path.

One of the songs went something like this:

"All of God's children have shoes. . .

In Heaven, Oh! In Heaven, they put on their shoes. . .

Oh in Heaven . . All of God's children have shoes."

The children smiled at this sweet lesson. I am sure they repeated the song as they walked the fields doing their chores. They sang the song as they walked miles to school. Often they had no shoes, or wore ones that were old and did not fit. But they thought sweetly of Heaven and of their sweet Mama. They learned of Great faith and of the journey to their Heavenly home. There was something much more important to these children, than just their own lot in life. There was a future and a reward, where they would have wonderful shoes and get to be with God.

There is a beautiful prayer many of us say each day; it is taken from Scripture (Matthew chapter 6). Part of it goes, "Our Father which art in Heaven, Hallowed be Thy name. Thy Kingdom Come. Thy will be done. In earth as it is in Heaven. Give us this day, our daily bread. . ." This prayer acknowledges that God takes care of us *today*, as the needs come. He may not always provide tomorrow's needs before it is necessary. Often, we impatient children pray for a need and expect it to suddenly appear. In this way, we are forgetting that it is not "OUR will" that must be done, but "HIS," and in His timing, *for His purposes*. (Romans 8:28)

We must have faith in Him, like a trusting child. We are grateful to be called His very own children, and we are happy to work here in His service. Sometimes, we must wait days, months, or years for our prayers to be answered. At other times, our prayers are answered in beautiful ways.

Mrs. C. H. Spurgeon suffered for most of her life as an invalid. But she did incredible work for the Lord. At times, her sickness and weariness caused her to pause and recover. But once she was better, she got right back to work. She was the wife of the beloved British Pastor, Charles Spurgeon. She was a loving mother of twin sons, and kept the home. She also faithfully did charity work (from home) to help other Pastors who suffered in want. God blessed her efforts greatly.

Sometimes her prayers were slow to be answered. Other times, the need was supplied before she realized it was necessary! There was a time when something she wanted (a "want" mind you), to cheer her. Just some sweet things, - an opal ring, and a singing bird. She only told her husband. They both laughed, thinking it was not possible. In those days, people were more practical and did not spend money on that which was frivolous. Oh, but the Lord heard that little prayer and worked through the Saints, who didn't even realize her request. These dear ones passed the little gifts on through Charles, as they were no longer needed in their own homes. And so it was that Mrs. Spurgeon got her ring and bird, to brighten her sick days. Charles said to his dear wife, something like, "I think you are one of God's spoiled children." And how dearly sweet and precious it was!

Our prayers are like songs that reach heaven. We may have dire needs, or little childish requests. Yet, when we trust our Heavenly father to meet those needs whether it be here on earth, or after we pass the gates of Heaven, and are content with HIS perfect will, we will be happy in heart. Our little songs and prayers, as we travel along this life, pass on sweet lessons to those around us because of our FAITH.

Just remember, whenever you may find your faith weakening, or your heart getting weary, remember that dear old mother who taught her little ones, that all of God's children have shoes.

Living on His Income

Frank and Dorothy's House (My Childhood Home)

Living on His Income

Living on His Income

Books by Mrs. White

(Available at Amazon.com)

Mother's Faith

For the Love of Christian Homemaking

Early Morning Revival Challenge

Mother's Book of Home Economics

Living on His Income

For more information or to find Mrs. White's books, please visit:

The Legacy of Home Press

http://thelegacyofhomepress.blogspot.com

Also see Mrs. White's blog:

http://thelegacyofhome.blogspot.com

Housewife:

A married woman who stays home.

This is a lifelong vocation.
It is an old-fashioned term,
and something to be proud of.

Not a "domestic engineer."
Not a "home manager."

An old fashioned housewife,
who keeps the home,
and abides there.

- Mrs. White

Living on His Income

Made in the USA
Middletown, DE
20 April 2018